ALL THAT JAZZ

Poems by Kevin Rabas

Kansas City   Spartan Press   Missouri

Spartan Press
Kansas City, Missouri
spartanpresskc.com

Copyright (c) Kevin Rabas 2017
First Edition 1 3 5 7 9 10 8 6 4 2
ISBN: 978-1-946642-07-3
LCCN: 2017931036

Design, edits and layout: Jason Ryberg
Author photo: Dave Leiker
Cover photo and design: Dave Leiker, Eric Sonnakolb
Saxophone loaned by P.J. Stephenson
All rights reserved. No part of this publication may be reproduced or transmitted in any form or by any means, electronic or mechanical, including photocopying, recording or by info retrieval system, without prior written permission from the author.

Prospero's Books and Spartan Press would like to thank Jeanette Powers, j.d.tulloch, Jason Preu, M. Scott Douglass, Shawn Pavey, Shawn Saving, Jesse Kates, Jim Holroyd, Steven H.Bridgens, Thomas Mason, Beth Dille, Mason Wolf, The West Plaza Tomato Co. and The Robert J. Deuser Foundation For Libertarian Studies.

The author gratefully acknowledges the editors of the following publications, in which versions of the following poems first appeared:

No Road Trip in The Greensboro Review,
Pool, Ring in Dunes Review,
Meeting Lisa in Otoliths,
You Sing? in Existere,
Plaintive Violins, Menningers Brought Us All to Topeka,
and *Governor's Dirt* in Tittynope,
On 'Skipping Skeletons' in Turtle Island

Thanks go to Katelyn Dorrell for her help revising and formatting this book. Her help was invaluable — and swift and thorough. Thanks to John Reynolds for helping me send some of these poems out into the world, sometimes in earlier versions.

Thanks go to Jason Ryberg for publishing this book. This would be a pile of papers in a manila folder, if not for him.

Thanks go to Dave Leiker for the excellent cover and author photography and to Eric Sonnakolb for the cover design.

Thanks, always, to Lisa Moritz for her unfailing, unflagging support. She keeps our house running, while I write. Thanks also to Eliot, who sometimes says, *Papa, are you writing this down? Stop.* Thanks to my parents, Gary and Joyce Rabas, and double thanks go to my mother for her strong copyediting eye and mind, without which this book would be more error-riddled.

Thanks to my poetic brother, Dennis Etzel, Jr, for his continuing friendship. He's seen and known these poems for months, years.

Thanks to a pack of literary friends, some far and some near, including Adrienne K. Goss, Joseph DeLuca, Amy Sage Webb, Jen Rae Hartman, Tyler Sheldon and Alexandria Arceneaux, Jim and Anna Ryan, Richard Warner, Mike Graves, Tracy Million Simmons, Cheryl Unruh, Marcia Lawrence, Robert L. Dean, Max McCoy, and Masami Sugimori.

Thanks to Sam and Alicia Styles for their planning and hospitality before and during our Carpinteria trip. (Thanks also go to Joyce and Gary on that account.)

CONTENTS

Jail Show / 1

Squirrel Traps / 2

Four Takes on a Phrase / 3

Moritz Kid Fourth / 5

Super Sense / 6

Philmont / 7

Philmont #2 / 8

Rain on the Mountain, Boy Scouts / 9

Tenth Year Reunion / 10

I'm Not / 11

Free-Range Chickens, Crisp Organic Farm / 12

Ordering Ma Po / 13

Position in Emporia / 14

Waking Late / 15

Water Problems / 16

Shrine Bowl / 17

No Road Trip / 18

Your Kiss / 19

Shatner Stops in Emporia / 20

Imagine We Loved Like Children / 21

You Sing? / 22

Not That Traditional / 23

At the New Year's Eve Gig at The Majestic,
   2000 / 24

At 20 / 25

Pit, Big River / 27

42 Regular / 28

At the Literary Awards; Or,
   Drum Roll, Please / 29

Marketing Pic, Chuck Haddix, Director,
>MARR Sound Archive, Summer 1997 / 30
Plaintive Violins / 31
Cello / 32
The Beats, Like Us / 33
Vitruvian Man / 34
Menningers Brought Us All to Topeka / 35
Governor's Dirt / 36
T— Rally / 37
Oncoming Darkness / 38
Caucusing for Hillary / 39
Autumn leaves, like script / 40
9/11 / 41
Tactile / 42
New York Rush / 43
Zumba / 44
Dr W's Power / 45
Dead Bird / 46
After American Portrait with One Eye
>by Fritz Scholder / 47
After Dartmouth Portrait No. 14
>by Fritz Scholder / 49
Skipping Skeletons #2
>painting by Allison Schulnik / 51
Skipping Skeletons #3 / 53
Skipping Skeletons #4 / 55
[How the red threads move to breath…] / 56
[How do you draw the self, the face…] / 57
After Eric Conrad's The Existentialist
>steel, hand-woven fabric, and found clothes / 58
Desert Flower, Carpinteria Beach / 59

For Lisa

Jail Show

Blind Klamm takes our group
   of kid magicians
to the county jail, where we
   thumb-cuff each other,
demonstrate escapes, our hands undone
   fast as metal clasps can click.
Show me how you do that, kid,
   says a guy on the inside.
Can't, we say. *It's part of the trick.*
Magician's code? he says.
Yes.
Ok, kid. That I understand.

Squirrel Traps

My sister, Alicia, says that's nice, you're trapping
squirrels and letting them loose in Shawnee Mission
Park, instead of Dad shooting them from the back
fence with his pellet gun. Sure, my Mom says, until
my sister catches Mom trotting across the lawn in
her high heels before work at the paper, trap in hand.
Mom drops that trap into a full 8-gallon bucket,
water lapping at the sides, and shoves a big rock
on top.

Four Takes on a Phrase

I.
Wednesday 13 December 2011 4:40 pm

Sixty degrees after two days of rain;
it's Indian summer in Emporia,
   and the clouds
behind Timmerman Elementary would look
just like a Hollywood backdrop
if they were not moving
   one mile an hour
north, a crawl of water,
   clouds like laborers
with thick white airport sacks,
   carrying something
Santa wants moved
   from workshop to sleigh,
from truck to chimney to Christmas tree.

II.
We have always run (from thunder)

A crawl of water, the clouds
like laborers with thick white airport sacks,
the storm behind a thunderhead,
anvil of hail and forked white lightning, and I run
the sidewalk home, sneaks in water, over and in
puddles, my hair a mop, my shirt a new slick skin,

lizard skin, water in my socks, a squish of shoes.
This is how the caveman must have lived, in one
(long) run; Water God above, land a place onto
which heaven dumped, dropped, shot, spat.

III.
crawl of water

DIVE WITH CAUTION
swim w/ death
beat me
off the blocks
if you can.

IV.
(Life) Guards, Storm

The pool's surface, a crawl of water,
lightning arcs above us, warring clouds,
and the lane lines snake quick across water,
ratchet in. Geoff runs the handle round,
and I hold the spool,

so it doesn't jump into water, sink. We roll them in.
Sarah paws ice from the snowcone machine, lobs
ice, August's snowballs; we dodge, jump, dive, zing
into water, forget weather, huddle
under dark water, come up
into white light.

Moritz Kid Fourth

Lighting fireworks
　with a blow torch,
throwing lady fingers
　into a water bucket.
With a boom,
　up the water shoots.

Super Sense

He sees their bones, hearts
   pumping. The world
is too much: every voice
   at once, pencils tapping,
clock hand ticking; teacher
   asks, *Clark, what's
wrong?* Being Superman
   is one big spell
of PTSD.

Philmont

My pack's 72 lbs, and I'm 120.
   Up the mountain we go.
Before, we cast off all
   we can: ½ a stick
of deodorant, a big fishing lure, half
   our matches, all but one pair
of shorts, shirts, socks. To eat,
   all you need are a bowl, cup, spoon.
The fork and knife can stay
   in camp 'til you return.

Philmont #2

We'd hiked 45 miles
        of a 75-mile trek,
and we had to go back,
  take another path home.
        McAndrews, with that
office job, had blisters
        on his feet. There were ten
of us scouts, all we needed
        in our packs: tents, food.
McAndrews picked at his feet
        in his tent, the rain coming down,
like God's whisper. So, needle in hand,
        we decided.

Rain on the Mountain, Boy Scouts

We wake in rain
  and say, *It's waterlogged*
  as Degobah
swamp in here, rain pooled
  three inches in the tent corner, CJ's
white-socked feet, soaked.
  We greet the dawn
blur-eyed, our glasses
  dotted with droplets.

Tenth Year Reunion

At the high school reunion, I carry an umbrella
   prop, social crutch, my eyes
wild. Days before, I got knocked down
   in a city game of hoops, hit my head,
couldn't complete the LSAT, turned to scribbling
   in journals, thick ones.

Thad, who kept his classy button-up collars popped in
geography, European History AP, who kept rewinding
Dances with Wolves when Dr. Z went out to smoke so that
we watched that flick seven classes. Thad, he mimed,
he mocked, he climbed the dance rail and made to jump,
pointing a digit out at me at the party.

I'm Not

The lady on the sidewalk,
        her face a twist
of leather, says
        Can you spare me three dollars
for my meds and I say,
        Sorry. I don't have
any cash, and I go
        to back my car out,
and she sees me
        edging along, trying to see
past a truck, and says,
        You're good, and I know
I'm not.

Free-Range Chickens, Crisp Organic Farm

On our farm, Farmer John Crisp says, *the chickens have the right of way.* We're in his golf cart touring the plot. A bigger chicken struts up, and John says, *He's the rooster, and we give him space. He protects the hens.*

There are orange New Hampshire Reds everywhere, a heritage breed, red on green, chickens in the grass. *The more they have access to sunlight and grasshoppers and room to move, the healthier they are, and the more they lay eggs.*

Chickens came across with the pilgrims, but originated in South America, he says, *and those first chickens laid blue-green eggs.* He says they now call them Americana, use them only on Easter, look, pre-colored eggs.

Ordering Ma Po

When I say I want
   Ma Po Tofu,
the waitress corrects my emphasis;
   hit the *Po* harder
   and the *Fu*.
On the ticket *To* and *Fu* are two
   separate words, perhaps
tofu is an Americanism, like
   the fortune cookie, a hard gold fold,
or General Tso
   with his orange chicken.

Position in Emporia

I'm alone in this little university town
        here on a temporary gig, the light
        golden in through these blinds
and onto my kitchen, my writing table,
        where I pen postcards
to my wife, now in another town
        more than an hour away
with our son, 2, who sees me
        once a month, if that much.
I buy him a ball or a disc or a little man,
        hope he remembers, hope he thinks
of me as he holds that plastic tight.
Will we both hold through autumn light?
        I grade a few papers
until darkness falls, shut the blinds,
        flip the lights to full,
put a few poems in the mail
        to my love and a few
to magazines. Perhaps this is how
        we hold, how we go.

Waking Late

That afternoon off, I pet the cat, wrote.
I planned some pages, made a big salad, sat
in silence. I didn't turn any music on.
I made a call. Got my teeth cleaned. Planned
to get my oil changed. I'd slept until 11.
And when I awoke, the world had been turning,
long and sidelong, and nothing waited up
for me, but I had that calm one has underwater,
those slow, smooth movements, that long
sure gaze, the sounds coming in as if through a
dream.

W 13 May 2015

Water Problems

I.
The rain begins
        again
Hope it don't
        leak.

II.
There's a sidewalk
        all around
our house now, sloped out.

Shrine Bowl

Night, beyond the dance floor,
        at the edge of the woods,
Shelly and I kiss, my hand
in her shirt. I'm so slow
with her buttons, with her bra,
like a sash underneath, and I'm 15,
lead drum line at camp,
        and when they catch us
that's the only reason
        they don't swiftly kick us both out.

No Road Trip

I know you said I could stay with you in your
parents' basement with your little daughter, make
the four-hour trip to St. Louis this Saturday, the long
blue road stretched out like the arch, and I want to
come, wish I could, but things have changed. Lucinda
kissed me last night, a hot butterfly kiss, drew me to
her, said she wants me here, and little Adam came in
and cuddled up with us, his blonde hair at our noses,
and we were, for a snap shot, a happy family, like the
cookie fortune says. We were beyond the desertions,
Lucinda leaving work her first day, gathering Adam
into her small red car and driving to KC, saying we're
through, my parents talking her back into it, into me,
and Lucinda arriving back home in her blue raincoat,
hair like an oil slick in the rain.

Your Kiss

     Your kiss,
that first hot tea sip,
and February with its blue-white fingers
     on my chest
cannot cool my heart,
     when your lips
hold my lips, like the very
     touch of summer,
that blonde, bold, golden light.

Shatner Stops in Emporia

William Shatner rides into town on his three-wheel motorcycle. Someone says he does this all the time, motorcycles a few miles with his posse, stops, eats and drinks, then gets in his touring van and rides the rest of the way. But there's some sort of trouble, so he has to motor about an hour and a half in the heat, 95-degree Kansas sun, and so *Shat* comes in sweat drenched, red-faced, heart-attack hot, and we look it up: he's 84; tough old dog, one time commander of a fleet starship.

Imagine We Loved Like Children

Z, she has strongman obsidian Will and I on one
foot, the other leg pretzeled around, yoga in city
park. Later, we'd eat potato soup, everything vegan,
everything communal, everything free. Z had honey-
comb dreds, blonde and amber, and she wrote like
Virginia Woolf when she wasn't teaching us how
to stand, breathe. I shared an office with her at the
university on the hill in Outpost of Progress row;
we'd lecture forever if we stayed. When I was in the
dark on hardwood floor in child pose, Z crept and
touched an arm. I flinched. It was a test. Should I
have held, stayed like rock, or should I have reached
out and taken hold? It was like we were naked, when
we were not. We lived within that Lennon tune,
Imagine. There were no boundaries, no religion,
but what we lived within a moment, and each action
led to everything or nothing, like touch, like kiss,
like spooning potatoes to the tongue. I loved *Z* like a
toddler would love another. I held out my hand once,
and she said, *You need to learn to see her,* but who
did she mean? Will, he walked off with *Z* at day's end,
the stars coming on, her hand in his hand, a trace of
grey potatoes on his lip.

You Sing?

Day takes me to his apartment to meet his out-of-town girl, who's asleep under blue silk sheets, he shows me. Day puts down his silver pistol on the stereo amp and plays me *Brasiliero,* which I've heard before, but the batucada drum corps rattles from those stereo holes out through the doors and into that shabby rusted four-floor elevator cage that we came up in, and out through cracked burgundy brick out into the KC night. This was once a nice part of town. Day's friend, a singer, rises. Or her head does, and her sheet spills to the floor. I've never seen a black woman naked. She's the most beautiful, shapely woman I've ever seen, of any color, and she doesn't seem to mind that I've seen. I try to play it cool, hand her the sheet, and she takes the edge slow and swishes the silk around her like water in a bath, says, *You're cute. Day tells me you can play. Swing funk?* Sure, I say. *Sing?* Nah, I say. *Come on,* she says, and starts in, *Sing with me,* and I'm choked up and fearful and shy; a goddess has asked me to sing, and I do, and she says, *You're right. You don't sing,* and that's it. She needed a drummer who could sing; we're done; and she closes her eyes and goes back under that blue silk sheet, and I remember the name of that Mingus tune, *Orange Was the Color of Her Dress, Then Blue Silk.* I go quietly down the stairs.

Not That Traditional

Bandleader Doris says, *The minister says she wants
our services to have a more traditional feel,* and I
know what she means, no drums, or drums set to
a Sousa march. Or worse, *tap tap tap*, brushes on
hi-hat or one big brush circle swish on snare, sound
of the turntable arm cycling, idling on the LP's inner
ring, monotony of background click, nothing doing,
and so I say, *You mean like we get a goat and
sacrifice it on an altar and raise the burnt offerings
up to the heavens?* And Doris says, *Not that traditional.*

At the New Year's Eve Gig at The Majestic, 2000

During break, an hour to tomorrow,
   bassist *Bear* sidles up to me
at the urinal, streams, and says,
   That's a nice tie. Silk?
I look at the tag. Nah, Rayon.
   *How come I don't have a tie
like that?* Want this one?
   *Nah, preppy. That's for you.
And your class.* My class?
   But I'm here playin' this gig
with you. *You don't need to.*
   How do you know? *That tie.
That tie's enough.*

At 20

Karrin calls
        on the red dorm phone,
                and I pick up.
My first big gig. Teacher's out of town,
        and Karrin heard me sit in and solo
at Plaza III, and called me over,
        said, *Kid, you've learned this language,*
and swapped cards.

She knows I'm not 21, says
        no one will know.
I pack my drums carefully
        as I can, cherry shells
in big black bags that zip,
        my hardware, those metal rods
in a ski bag, what I can afford.
        I put in more hours
behind the kit, watch my hands,
        arms in the mirror, work form,
and play low, stay soft,
        but still burn, hit, stick, attack.

At the gig, I can hang, keep up,
        find the pocket and sit in it.

Karrin grins, stops looking
>back, and sings like on any other
purple night, and the guys pat me
>on the back, when they go to drink,
Doin' fine.

Second set, thick Richard Ross sits in,
>wearing African rags, his voice
like his chest and belly,
>full, gold. And the townies
show up, the half blind drummer
>with Coke bottle specs,
Southpaw with his black leather vest,
>who tries to razz me, says, *How old?*
and calls the bar to card me,
>who do, who let me play
that last set, but say, *Not him. Not again.*

Milt says, *Ok, son,* and kicks *Big Wind,*
>song he sings, moans
to low bass notes, and I swift quick
>on brushes, just me and him,
and Karrin gives me
>the thumbs up, pushes
the check into my pocket, says,
>>*Next year, young man.*

Pit, *Big River*

My mother brought me a coconut,
        and my father cut that nut in two
with the circular saw. I helped.
        There are horse hoof clops
in *Big River*, and I'm on
        percussion in the pit, 15,
on one of my first orchestra gigs,
        community theatre in the KC suburbs,
what to do with a summer.

42 Regular

At 42 regular, my brown suede sportscoat is a little
too large, coat from my return to jazz, neon nights,
cymbal snare, and low tom nights, amber sax
purplings, head injured, unable to read, teach;
coat in which I sewed a hundred dollar bill,
a trick I learned from reading Li-Young Lee, exile,
poet, lost, fled from his homeland;
my life is so much smaller than his.

At the Literary Awards; Or, Drum Roll, Please

When I get to the room,
  the Kansas Poet Laureate is at the stand,
testing the mic, and I'm here having lost
  to him, packing in my drums, and he asks
if I'm the entertainment, says play me a rim shot
  when I joke, and I say, *"Cheesy as it is,*
I've been asked to play drum rolls
  for winners." "Really?" he says.
I play one for him.

Marketing Pic, Chuck Haddix, Director, MARR Sound Archive, Summer 1997

I haul this big X-metal base construction site light
I borrowed from my father and illuminate a row of
Chuck's archive LPs, ask Chuck to stand by a favorite
title or two, and he leans an elbow on the shelf like
a late-night DJ resting his head, and I turn the knob
and click Chuck into silver, into acetone, into Tri-X
film frame, using my 1930s Rolei. I'll always see him
like this.

Plaintive Violins

How violins pull
        the tenderer emotions,
like running a spoon lure
        through calm water,
with a little spin, and like pulling
        marionette strings
on a long-limbed puppet,
        a puppet that's slow
dancing with another
        spindly, upright puppet.

Cello

Sit too close
        to the cello,
and that bow
        across strings
may pull
        tears, clench
your stomach, gut,
        make you breathe
like a man on a beach
        near drowned.
Music can do that to you,
        open you to the salt breeze,
open you to the clouds
        and the thin fingers of the sun.

The Beats, Like Us

The Beats were separated
        by time, by miles,
and they spent their lives
        hitching, hiking
to reunite, and in between:
        the writing.
(Like us.)

Vitruvian Man

At the lat pull-down, the pink-skinned
man in the burgundy muscle shirt,
custom-cut, scissored to fit, moves
like Da Vinci's *Vitruvian Man,* one man
in one plane, revealing just how far
a man, a woman, can stretch, can pull
at sinew and tissue, muscle and bone, the body
a mobile, a constellation, a set of planets, stars.

Menningers Brought Us All to Topeka

Over pink steak in the faculty lounge
   on the poet's night out
Avery says, *Menningers brought us all
   to town. My father worked there,* and Mechery
says his mother did. Everyone in psychology,
   psychiatry. What I don't tell them
is I'm also here because of Menningers,
   white-wall prison for the cloudy-minded.
I spent my night there, then drew up papers.
   It's crazy to stay, too crazy to stay.

Governor's Dirt

I pull a weed out of a driveway crack, get a little
   dirt under my nails, remember
how Governor Sam Brownback has a jar
   of dirt from the family farm, has a little bit
of dirt put under   his nails
   when they're manicured each week,
touch of home, touch of work, touch of dirt.

T— Rally

If you look out
  at your crowd,
your mouth to the mic,
  and they're beating someone,
fists to his face, feet
  to his ribs, know
you've turned bad bad bad,
  your voice
gone wrong, your soul
  split, spilt, spoiled, a mush.
Look up. God may not
  spite you with a golden
bolt, but I might,
  I just might.

Oncoming Darkness

Election night, autumn turns cold, on comes the first
hard freeze, / and the long dark roots make
their last reach for water before winter, / before the
darkness of the year.

Wednesday, 9 November 2016, 12:18 am, Emporia, Kansas

Caucusing for Hillary

Take my lunch late, vote
 for Hillary *(I'm with her)*
at the courthouse, one of five
 in line.
I caucused for her
 this time, last time,
my wife home with our young son:
 Who would you choose:
Barack, Hillary? and she said
 Hillary, and so I've voted
for her twice.

That may mean
 little to you,
but in this small red town,
 it's something, like a felony,
a hair lip, a bastard son,
 a three-legged dog.

Autumn leaves, like script

Autumn leaves, few
      to a branch,
like cursive script, the nib
      leaves a jagged,
blotted edge.

9/11

   After
we look up.
   Nothing.
Even in KS, not even
   birds
go overhead.

Tactile

Run a hand
  over limestone, ocean
all dried up.

Touch rust
  gingerly. Its wings,
its mushroom rims
  want skin.

New York Rush

Leonard says, you know how it is in New York.
You're first onto the subway platform, and you wait
and you wait and the platform fills with people, and
when the train comes, you have to push your way on
or the train leaves and you're left still standing on
the platform as the train pulls away.

Zumba

The women dance,
   arms up and out,
hand weights fisted; the nose points,
   and the body goes,
bent easily as pampas shoots,
    and hair like pampas plumes.

Dr W's Power

That's my power, my psychiatrist says, pointing
        to the fizz in his seltzer, the bubbles
swarming, rising. He must bring air up
        to where it breaks, dissolves
pops free and new up to the ceiling and to the
        clouds.

Dead Bird

Like a triangle, the bent leg
        of a baby bird, a clump
smashed on the sidewalk.

Eliot pokes it
        with a stick.
Flies rise.

We all come
        to an end.

After *American Portrait with One Eye* by Fritz Scholder

I.
The black paint
  drips from the broken, poked
eye; the face, purple;
the head-
  feather aslant,
askant. I see
  better this way.

II.
The drips
  on my face —
paint, not rain.

III.
Even after
  our artist
passes, I'll still be
  looking at you.

IV.
Mouth shut,
  a green line.
I don't smile
  for just anyone.

V.
Some say red, but I
  am purple
with red around.

VI.
Feather cocked flat
  to the horizon line,
    the sun
sets at my back.

After *Dartmouth Portrait No. 14* by Fritz Scholder

I.
My mask
  shows my teeth
for me, my own
  lips closed.
I wait, I watch
  through other eyes.

II.
Arm band, iron band,
  I feel the sun
along my arm, long
  after pale fire
sets.

III.
Some call me ugly,
  but that's
a mask.

IV.
When paint rains
　on me,
it's black.

V.
Look how much
　I've eaten,
how well
　I stand.

Skipping Skeletons #2
    painting by Allison Schulnik

I.
So much love
    when we run
through flowers
    between peonies,
your toes
    in marigolds.

II.
Can he catch me
    between the petals
and stems, the thorns and pistils —
flowers, what we run.

III.
Although we're mostly
    bones, you've
still got your tongue.

IV.
I will not wait
    for you, anyone.
When I run,
    I run —
past petals, past stems.

V.
She painted us thick,
> so we'd stick
to wood, to wall,
> to the heart.

VI.
I'd like to feel
> your hair again
in my hands, in my
> bones.

VII.
I loved you, alive,
> I love you, dead.
I'll love you
> in whatever
> afterlives that come.

CODA.
I'd pick you a rose,
> but I'm too busy
running after you.

Skipping Skeletons #3

I.
When we run
   I watch
the small of your back,
   and I run
until I can
   no longer.

II.
I can see
   into your ribs
and out
   to where
      your hands pump,
your fists loose, your body
   an open book.

III.
If only I could read you
   like this in life,
know your heart,
   your lungs,
      your mind,
a river spun.

IV.
We're no longer
 men, women,
we're bones.

Skipping Skeletons #4

What's left of your hair
　I watch, follow,
our fleshier parts
　gone.

A few teeth
　left, I use them
to woo you.

[How the red threads move to breath…]

How the red threads move
  to breath,
how the porcelain layers
  open, soft maw, clam-like
as if taking in water, air, light.

on Stephanie Lanter's "Preoccupy"
  porcelain, underglaze, glaze, thread, wire, 2016

[How do you draw the self, the face…]

How do you draw
   the self, the face,
but shoot your eyes
   with the camera, come back
with your pencils and catch
   what the camera misses, the colors,
how they go, like dots,
   like hairs, like those ghosts
of glare photographers call
   spectral highlights.

On Derek Wilkinson's "Self-Portrait Frowning"
   and "Self-Portrait Smiling"
pastel and charcoal on paper, 2016

After Eric Conrad's *The Existentialist*
  steel, hand-woven fabric, and found clothes

None of these clothes
  fit, a bag of rags,
color bundle, a creature w/ a glitter
  snout, fox head, cloud nose,
with scent of street & dirt & drink.

Desert Flower, Carpinteria Beach

Eliot, just 13, picks a pink flower from an ice plant,
its center about the size of a quarter, like a cactus
bloom, but bigger, its pink petals wiry and curved
like eyelashes. He says, *for mama.* We bring the
flower back to our hotel room, after a few hours in
our trunk, and forget to put that flower in water,
but the flower doesn't seem to mind, a desert plant,
a succulent, it lasts without water the whole week,
bloomed perfectly, as if untouched, placed atop our
TV. Like memory, like vacation pictures or travelogue
jots, that flower lasts. Each morning mother puts her
nose to its petals, says, *beautiful,* and, *thank you,
little one,* and Eliot smiles big, but we all know that
flower holds no scent, never does, never did. But what
it holds is magic; transitory, travel magic. Only we
don't need to take it, when we go. We leave that flower
on top of a small stack of change and bills for someone
else to pick up.

Kevin Rabas chairs the Department of English, Modern Languages, and Journalism at Emporia State and leads the poetry and playwriting tracks. He has eight books, including *Bird's Horn*, *Lisa's Flying Electric Piano*, a Kansas Notable Book and Nelson Poetry Book Award winner, *Sonny Kenner's Red Guitar*, also a Nelson Poetry Book Award winner, *Green Bike*, *Eliot's Violin*, *Late for Cymbal Line*, *Spider Face: stories*, and *Songs for My Father: poems & stories*. Rabas writes regularly for Kansas City's *Jazz Ambassador Magazine* (JAM). Rabas's plays have been produced across Kansas and in North Carolina and San Diego. His work has been nominated for the Pushcart Prize five times, and Rabas is the winner of the Langston Hughes Award for Poetry, the Victor Contoski Poetry Award, the Jerome Johanning Playwriting Award, and the Salina New Voice Award.

www.ingramcontent.com/pod-product-compliance
Lightning Source LLC
Chambersburg PA
CBHW021451080526
44588CB00009B/791